PUFFIN BOOKS

WELL, WELL, WELL:
ALL ABOUT HEALTH

This is a book about YOU. It's also a book about
EVERY BODY! It will help you to find out how
every part of your body works together to keep
you healthy – from your brain to your bones, your
heart to your nose. It will also help you to
understand what happens when your body
doesn't work so well, and the people and places
that can make you better. There are some
amazing facts about your body too: did you know
that there's enough water in your body to fill up
four pairs of wellington boots? Dr Pete's top tip
on how to swallow the medicine as well as hints
for keeping yourself, and others, healthy and fit
are covered in this Young Puffin Fact Book.

Peter Rowan has appeared as Dr Pete on
TV-am's *Wide Awake Club* as well as on BBC
Radio's *Cat's Whiskers*. He is medical
correspondent for the *Early Times* and medical
expert for BBC Schools Radio. He lives with his
wife Margaret, daughter Sarah and son Edward
in Norfolk, where he is a family doctor.

WELL, WELL, WELL
ALL ABOUT HEALTH

Dr Peter Rowan

ILLUSTRATED BY
Jane Cope

PUFFIN BOOKS

*For the children
of Tivetshall School*

PUFFIN BOOKS

Published by the Penguin Group
Penguin Books Ltd, 27 Wrights Lane, London W8 5TZ, England
Viking Penguin, a division of Penguin Books USA Inc.
375 Hudson Street, New York, New York 10014, USA
Penguin Books Australia Ltd, Ringwood, Victoria, Australia
Penguin Books Canada Ltd, 2801 John Street, Markham, Ontario,
Canada L3R 1B4
Penguin Books (NZ) Ltd, 182–190 Wairau Road, Auckland 10,
New Zealand

Penguin Books Ltd, Registered Offices: Harmondsworth, Middlesex,
England

First published 1990
10 9 8 7 6 5 4 3 2 1

The moral right of the author has been asserted

Printed in England by Clays Ltd, St Ives plc
Filmset in Linotron Century Old Style

Contents

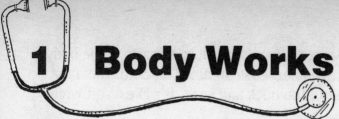

1 Body Works

Your body is an amazing living machine. All its many parts work together to keep you healthy, as you grow up and live your life.

THE BRAIN AND NERVES

The brain controls your body. It's a soft grey and white computer inside your head. This control centre is probably the most important organ of all.

7

Nerves run out from it to all parts of the body. The main nerve is contained inside the spinal bones of the neck and back. It's like a soft white rope.

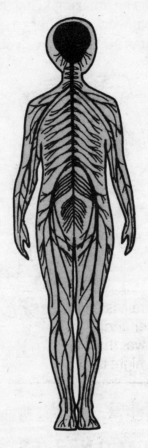

Messages come and go from the brain as if it were a giant telephone exchange. This particular telephone exchange has millions and millions of connecting lines.

You stand on a nail, and in a split second nerves running from the foot have 'told' the brain. The brain then tells the leg muscles to lift that foot up quickly.

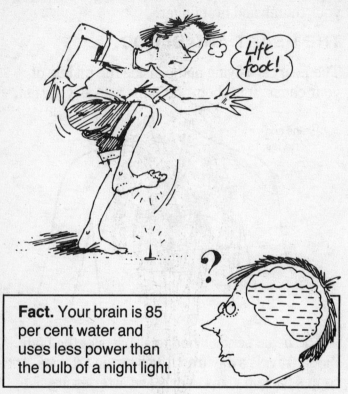

Fact. Your brain is 85 per cent water and uses less power than the bulb of a night light.

Here are three experiments to show some of the ways your brain works.

1 Add two and two. The brain is thinking.

2 Stick your tongue out. The brain tells the muscles of the mouth to move.

9

3 You are touching this book. The brain and nerves 'feel' the paper and tell you what it's like. Can your brain tell the difference between one page and two pages of this book? Feel between your thumb and first finger.

THE HEART AND BLOOD

The heart is a living pump inside the middle of your chest. It is about the same size as your fist.

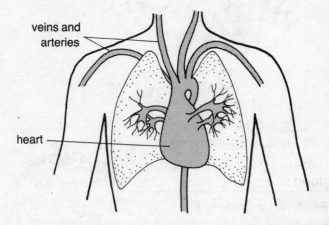

veins and arteries

heart

The heart sends blood to all parts of the body. Blood travels away from the heart in arteries, and comes back in veins. Veins and arteries are like small pipes.

When the blood returns to the heart, the body has used up its oxygen, so the heart sends the blood to the lungs to get some more. The lungs reload it with oxygen from the air breathed in, and then the heart pumps it off again around the body.

Here are a few 'heart sums' to work out with a calculator. (The answers are given at the foot of the page.) As you sit reading this book your heart is beating about seventy times a minute, so . . .

1 How many times is that in an hour?

2 How many times in a day?

3 How many times in a week?

If your calculator has room for only eight numbers you can't go much further. Let me tell you that in a lifetime your heart will beat about 2,500,000,000,000 times!

Blood is nearly all water. Red cells give it its colour, and there are five million of them in every pinprick of blood. These cells have iron in them. This helps carry oxygen to the body when you breathe it in.

Answers: 1. 4,200; 2. 100,800; 3. 705,600.

There are white cells too in blood. Their job is to fight germs. You see them when you have a boil. The white centre of the spot is the white cells that are fighting for you!

> **Fact.** If all your blood vessels were joined end to end, they would go around the world.

THE DIGESTIVE SYSTEM –
The inside story of a food processor!

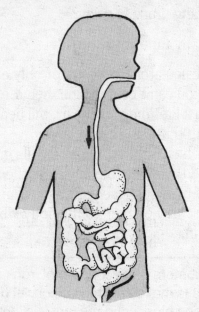

When you chew food in your mouth and swallow it, it passes down into your stomach and then along the coiled tubing of your intestines. (If laid out straight, your insides would be about the

Tallest giraffe

same length as the school bus, or as tall as the tallest giraffe. Just as well they're coiled up inside you!)

Some of the food eaten is used by the body to help you grow. Some is used to give you energy to do things like run around the playground. Some travels straight through you and goes down the toilet a day or two later.

Your body is made up of what you eat and drink. This is why it is so important not to eat junk food.

THE LUNGS AND BREATHING

The lungs are inside the ribcage of your chest. There is one on the right side and one on the left side. (The heart is between them.) They are like pink sponges with lots of tiny air spaces. A large air tube from your nose and mouth brings fresh air with oxygen to all these spaces when you breathe in.

Breathing allows the two lungs to bring this oxygen into the blood for the heart to pump around the body.

Here are some different ways air goes in and out of your lungs.

Breathing
When you are resting, you take air in and out of your lungs about twelve times every minute.

Speaking
Your voice is made by air leaving your lungs past two vocal cords in your throat. These vibrate like an elastic band.

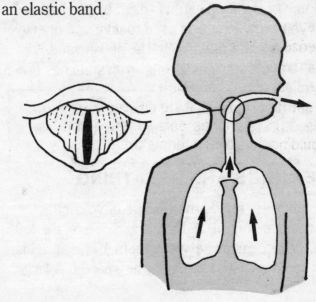

Yawning

A yawn is simply an extra big breath in.

Experiment: sit opposite a friend and yawn. See how long before your friend yawns too. No one knows why yawns are 'catching'. I bet you've started yawning just reading this – and not because you're bored!

Laughing

A laugh is a long breath out with some 'h' noises added in. Try it and see.

Hiccuping

A hiccup is a quick breath in.

Coughing

A cough is a very quick blast of breath out.

Sneezing

A sneeze is like a cough but it is faster and goes out of the nose.

Breathtaking Fact. If the millions of air spaces in your lungs were flattened out, they would nearly cover a tennis court.

Three things you can't do!

1 Talk normally while you breathe in.

2 Sneeze with your eyes open.

3 Pinch your nose and hum.

MUSCLES, BONES AND JOINTS

Bones are the framework of the body on which everything else hangs. There are over 200 bones altogether.

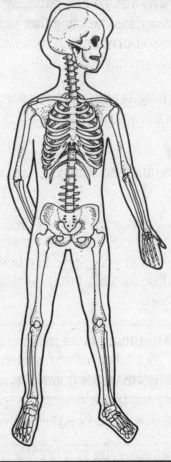

> **Fact.** A quarter of the bones in your body are found in your feet.

In places there are joints between the bones which can be moved by muscles. You can move some muscles yourself – for example, those in your hand when you write, and those in your legs when you walk, and you use over 200 to run! Other muscles, like the ones that make your heart beat and your stomach rumble, move without you even having to think.

Facts about muscles

1 The biggest muscle in the body is the one you sit on.

2 You use seventeen muscles to smile and forty-three to look sad. So save energy and smile!

3 There are over 600 muscles in your body – three times as many as there are bones.

WATER

Water is one of the most important parts of you. When you drink a glass of water, it soon goes into your blood. As the water goes in, so it's also taken out by your two kidneys. Your bladder stores it until – with luck! – you are near a toilet.

> **Fact.** There's enough water in your teacher's body for you to have a bath in, or to fill an elephant's trunk.

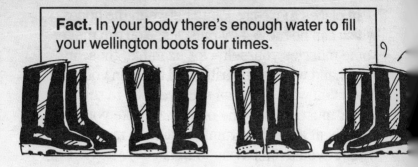

Fact. In your body there's enough water to fill your wellington boots four times.

SKIN

Skin keeps you healthy in many ways. It keeps germs out. It keeps your body's water in. It also keeps other water out, so you can swim and walk in the rain without getting soggy.

It has an 'overcoat' of fat which will keep you warm in winter. And in summer, when things get hot, it can sweat and cool you off. It also has nerve endings, which allow you to touch and feel.

Skin is being worn away and replaced from underneath all the time. You get a complete new skin about once a month.

Fact. The outer layer of your skin is DEAD. It will have come off and been shed within a week. So when you kiss someone, you are in fact kissing dead tissue. Not a very romantic thought!

2 When Things Go Wrong

Good health means having a sound body and mind. There are bound to be times during your life when something goes wrong with the workings of your body. There are a lot of ways this can happen. You may fall and break a bone. A part of the body may get infected with a germ. You may even be born with something which affects your health.

Diseases, illnesses and accidents can usually be put right with medical help. And often medical help isn't even needed. The body has its own excellent ways of fighting disease.

This young boy's body bleeds very easily if he cuts himself. It takes a long time for the blood to stop flowing. He was born like this.

This mother has become very ill with worry because her new baby is not well.

The girl in the ambulance is being taken to hospital after being involved in a crash.

Leukaemia is a sort of blood cancer. Special treatment is given in hospital.

This child has an ear infection as a result of catching a cold. The family doctor is checking to see what is wrong before deciding on the best medicine.

This girl has asthma in the summer. She is using an inhaler to help her breathing.

This man is having an operation. A surgeon is cutting out his appendix. It became red and hot and made him sick with pain in his stomach. Another doctor works with the surgeon. She has put the patient into a deep sleep so that no pain is felt during the operation.

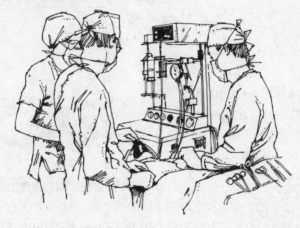

Good food and exercise are important for good health. Many millions of children in the world become ill through lack of food.

An old man uses a walking frame to help him get around his home and to the shops. Some of his bones are worn with age; he's not as young as he used to be.

Everyone has to put up with being sick at some time. When you are first ill, there are all sorts of ways people around you can notice something is wrong. Someone may see that you do not look well. Sometimes you may be able to say what's wrong, or how you feel.

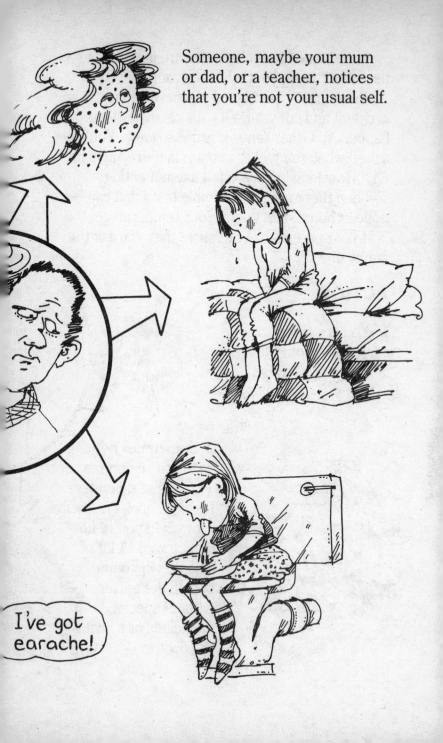

Someone, maybe your mum or dad, or a teacher, notices that you're not your usual self.

I've got earache!

After someone realizes you are not well, it's necessary to find out what is wrong.

Sometimes – perhaps if you have had an accident and cut yourself – it's clear what has happened. Other times it is not so easy. You'll be asked what you feel is wrong. 'Is there any pain?' Or, 'How long have you felt like not eating?'

Then there are some simple tests that can be done at home, like taking your temperature.

If your parents are not sure, they can ask the family doctor.

ACTION

1 You are given something from the home medical chest.

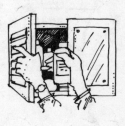

2 Sometimes nothing needs to be done except TLC – that's Tender Loving Care! TLC helps a lot when you're not feeling well. A lot of illnesses in young people get better without special medicines or a visit to the doctor.

3 Lots of parents have books – written by doctors – which they can use at home to look up advice.

4 A lot of minor accidents can be looked after very well at home – perhaps running a burnt finger under a cold tap.

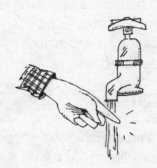

5 You are put to bed. Bed is a comfortable place to be when you're ill.

6 Your parents may decide to call the doctor out. Or you may be taken to the local surgery.

3 Teamwork

If your body does not get better on its own, or with help from the family medical chest, then there are teams of people ready to help.

DOCTORS

Doctors spend years studying diseases in people, and how to put any problems right. First they ask questions about what's wrong and then they examine the sick person.

Your doctor will be the sort of doctor who looks after families. His or her surgery is probably quite close to your home. Other doctors work in hospitals. Their work is different from the family doctor's. They may look after only young children, or do X-rays, or perform operations. The family doctor can send patients to these hospital doctors if further help is necessary.

NURSES

Nurses look after the general care of sick people. Nursing is a very skilled job because patients have to be watched carefully and any important changes in health reported to the doctor.

MIDWIVES

Midwives are nurses who look after mothers who are having babies.

AMBULANCE WORKERS

Ambulances are used to move sick people. Sometimes this must be done quickly when a very ill patient is rushed to hospital. Ambulance workers often work in twos. One drives and the other looks after the person who is ill in the back.

The ambulance has a siren to warn other drivers that it's in a hurry. The driver of the ambulance can switch this on and off as needed.

DENTISTS

Dentists look after the care of teeth and gums. A lot of their time is spent keeping people's mouths healthy. They don't spend all their time filling teeth!

> **Fact.** 200 to 300 years ago teeth were taken out by blacksmiths and shoemakers.

HEALTH VISITORS

Health visitors are special nurses who look after the health of whole families. They visit homes to check all is well, and take special care to watch over young children and the very old.

PHYSIOTHERAPISTS

Physiotherapists treat illness in physical ways, such as by massage and warmth, and by teaching exercises. When someone breaks a leg, a white hard plaster cast may be used to fix the break in place. When the bones have healed and the plaster is off, the physiotherapist teaches exercises to make the leg muscles strong again.

DIETITIANS

Dietitians tell people which foods are best for them. Some people are made ill by some foods and they must be taught to avoid them. Some people are too fat and need help to eat less food.

SPEECH THERAPISTS

Speech therapists teach patients to overcome problems with speaking. This girl has a stutter. She is being taught how to speak clearly.

There are many other people with important jobs in hospitals and doctors' surgeries: pharmacists who give you your medicine and tell you how to take it, porters who move patients around hospital, cooks and cleaners, laundry workers and those who answer phones and arrange for the doctor to see patients.

WHAT HAPPENS WHEN YOU SEE THE DOCTOR?

When the doctor sees you because you are ill, there are only two things that have to be done.

1 The doctor must find out what is wrong.

2 He or she must then put it right.

What's wrong?
Finding out what the matter is begins with the

doctor asking all sorts of questions about the problem, and then examining you.

Imagine you have been having trouble getting your breath because of asthma.

Does this happen when you run at school sports?...in the summer when there are lots of plants around? ...in bed at night?... when you touch the cat?...when you have a cold?

Examination. In this case the doctor listens to the patient's chest, and then asks her to blow into a tube. This test measures how fast she is able to blow air out.

Putting it right

After this the doctor is able to tell exactly what is wrong and can put things right.

'Your breathing's being affected by pollen from plants and it's made worse when you've got a cold. The medicine in this inhaler will stop the breathing problem. You'll need to take it during the summer.'

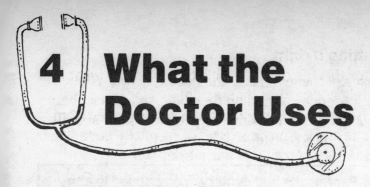

4 What the Doctor Uses

STETHOSCOPE

A stethoscope is used for listening to the sounds inside the human body. Using a stethoscope allows the doctor to hear the heart, the lungs and other parts inside the body working.

It usually has two rubber tubes. One end of each of these fits into the doctor's ears. When the other end is placed on the body, sounds can be picked up from inside the patient. These sounds pass down the tubes and can be heard.

Fact. In the last century doctors used to carry their stethoscopes under their top hats.

You can make your own stethoscope using a cardboard tube. The man who invented the first one in 1819 used a roll of paper.

Find a cardboard tube. The middle of a kitchen roll or toilet roll is fine. Place one end, as shown, on the bare chest of a friend. The room should be

lub-dub, lub-dub

quiet as the heart sounds are not loud. Place your ear over the other end of the tube. Listen carefully and you will hear a sound like two soft thuds, as if someone is saying 'lub-dub' quietly over and over again. This is the sound of the heart beating. It's the same sound that the doctor listens to.

Using a stethoscope and a special pump, the doctor can measure the pressure of the blood being pumped from the heart. It's important to check that the pressure doesn't rise too high.

LIGHTS

There are special lights for looking in eyes and ears.

This special light can look down your ear to see why you have earache.

With this one the doctor can look right to the back of the eyeball.

38

THERMOMETER

This measures the temperature of the body. If the temperature goes up – as it often does with infections – or down, then the doctor needs to know.

X-RAYS

X-ray machines take pictures like a camera. The X-rays can travel through skin and the flesh underneath but are stopped by bone, so an X-ray will show up a broken bone.

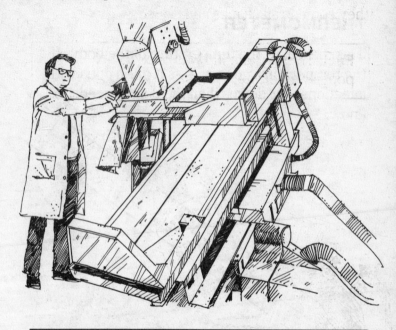

Fact. When X-rays were first invented, some people thought they were very rude and revealing! X-rays look inside the body, of course, but some thought they would simply show pictures of people with no clothes on! Special 'X-ray-proof' underclothes went on sale which, it was said, would not let X-rays through and let this happen.

MEDICINES

Some people think that taking medicines is the only way that ill people get better. This is not true. There is certainly not a pill for every ill. But medicines do make many illnesses better. And they come in all shapes and sizes.

> **Fact.** Tomato ketchup was once a very popular medicine.

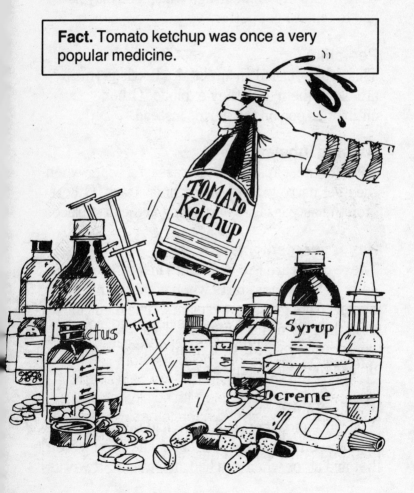

All medicines can be very dangerous if taken in the wrong way or by the wrong person. They are often kept in bottles which very young children cannot open. Young people should never take them unless they are given by a grown-up.

There is still a lot to learn about how drugs work. Here are some drugs which you may have had to take to get better.

Penicillin
This drug is called an antibiotic. It kills germs by attacking them until they explode! Other antibiotics poison the germs instead.

Asthma inhalers
Some of these make the air passages wider when they get narrow during an asthma attack. Others stop the air passages narrowing in the first place.

Hay fever medicines
These drugs are like defenders in football or netball. Hay fever starts when you breathe in pollens from grasses and plants. The medicines stop the pollens harming you. Take them as the doctor tells you. Most of them will not work unless they are taken correctly.

Paracetamol
You will almost certainly have had this medicine at some time or other. Perhaps when you were hot and ill, or when you had an earache. It works

in the brain, stops pain and cools you down. Paracetamol is an excellent medicine for making you better. Sadly it can taste horrible unless given another flavour!

Fact. Medicines are discovered in all sorts of ways. Many come from plants, but one was made from rocket fuel!

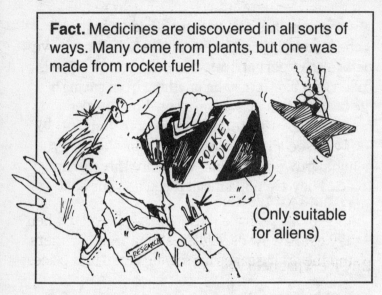

(Only suitable for aliens)

A lot of other very good medicines don't taste very nice! Grown-ups will often tell you that the best medicines taste the worst to get you to take them! Although there is truth in this, doctors have now found ways of making most of them taste better – while they make you better.

Dr Pete's Top Tip – if you have to take medicine you don't like, suck a peppermint first. Its strong flavour will hide the unpleasant taste of the medicine.

5 First Aid

If someone has an accident or suddenly becomes ill, you may be able to help them before an expert arrives. The help you can give is called first aid. It may be anything from saving a life to sticking a plaster on a cut. You can also help yourself if something happens to you.

If you see an accident or emergency and there is not a grown-up around, there are three things to do. They are not difficult if you do your best and keep calm.

1 Find out what has happened.

2 Give what help you can.

3 Get help.

WHAT'S HAPPENED?

Sometimes this is easy. You can see a hand cut on a piece of broken glass, and if you can't, the person with the cut will probably soon tell you!

But sometimes you may find someone who is not speaking. They are unconscious. Have they fallen out of a tree and been knocked out, or been taken ill with a mystery illness? This makes finding out what has happened more difficult.

GIVE HELP

This will depend on what is wrong. The best way
to learn first aid is in practical classes. Both the
Red Cross and St John Ambulance run classes for
young people.

GET HELP

This is very often the most important thing you
will do. It may be that you will get a teacher or a
grown-up who is near by. Telephones can be a
good, quick way to get help.

When reporting an accident by phone, dial 999,
or tap out 999 firmly if it is a push-button phone.
You do not need any money.

The person who answers will ask you which service you want – most commonly fire brigade, police or ambulance.

If you do not know which, you should just say what has happened.

Give your phone number if you can.

Wait until you are put through to the right person.

Tell the person on the other end WHO you are. Tell them slowly and clearly WHAT has happened. Tell them WHERE you are and where the trouble is.

Do not put the phone down until you are told to.

Remember, people's lives depend on this sort of telephone call, so be sensible.

Fact. 999 was chosen as the emergency number for good reasons. It is easy to remember in a hurry, and using the same numbers makes it easier to dial in the dark.

QUIZ

Here's a quiz. See how you would get on if someone needed your help. Only one answer is right.

A friend cuts her hand in the playground. Would you:

   1 Put a dock leaf on the cut and tell her to run home?

   2 Hold the hand up, press a clean handkerchief on the cut and then get help?

   3 Give her another friend's medicine?

2 is right. Never take medicines without asking a grown-up. The cut should be kept clean, not have a dock leaf put on it. Pressing a clean dressing on to the cut will help stop the bleeding.

Your mum falls down the stairs at home and can't move because she thinks her leg is broken. Would you:

   1 Try to keep calm and go and tell a grown-up near by what has happened?

   2 Ask your mum to try and get up?

   3 Give her a drink of water?

1 is right. If you have a phone and know how to use it, you can also get help by dialling 999. It is wrong to move anyone who has had an accident and may have a broken bone. Do not give an injured person anything to eat or drink until it is clear what has happened, because this may delay treatment in hospital.

You burn your finger on a hot cooker.
Would you:

1 Run the burn under a cold tap?

2 Prick any blisters that come up?

3 Put butter on it?

1 is right. The cold water will take some of the pain away until you can get more help. Do not prick a blister as it could let germs into the burn through the broken skin. Putting butter on is a waste of time – and butter.

A friend faints in the classroom while you are waiting for the teacher to arrive.
Would you:

1 Slap her on the face?

2 Try and give her a drink of water?

3 Lay her gently down and raise her legs, then see that someone gets the teacher?

3 is right. Lifting the legs helps blood return to the heart and speed recovery. If there is any difficulty breathing, place the friend on one side to help keep breathing normal. Loosen any tight clothing around the neck.

Never give an unconscious person anything to drink in case they choke. Slapping her face is unkind and will not help at all.

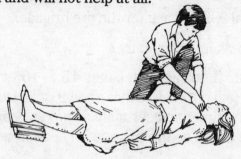

Someone in your class swallows some dinner money.
Would you:

1 Tell them they should try and be sick?

2 Tell a teacher what has happened?

3 Forget all about it because the coin will pass down the toilet?

2 is right. It's bad news to put things like this in your mouth. (Just as you should not poke things anywhere into your body.) If this happens, get help quickly. It may be that an X-ray at hospital will be needed to see where the dinner money is. Do not try and get them to be sick. It will not help, and they might simply choke. The coin will probably pass in a couple of days, but it might stick, so tell a grown-up.

You see smoke coming from a house in your street. There is a phone box near by.
Would you:

1 Go and get a bucket of water?

2 Dial 999 and ask for the fire brigade?

3 Break into the house?

2 is right. (Look again at pages **45 & 46**, where you can find out how to make a 999 call.) Do not waste any time, and certainly do not go near a possible fire. The fire brigade is needed – and quickly.

6 Hospital

A hospital is a place to care for the sick and wounded. Not everyone who visits a hospital has to stay in. Many well people go there, just to check that all is fine. You may need to stay – for example, if you have your tonsils out – but often going to hospital means just going to see a doctor in a clinic.

There are wards where sick people are looked after in beds by nurses and doctors.

There are many special tests done in hospitals. This man is having his heart checked.

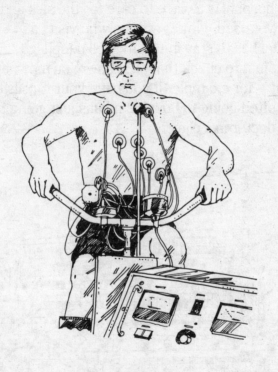

There are special wards to look especially carefully after the very sick.

There are clinics where doctors look at people to help the family doctor.

X-ray pictures of the body can be taken in hospital.

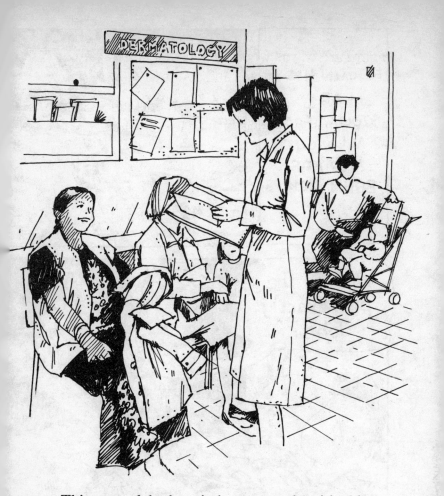

This part of the hospital sees people with skin problems.

Operations are usually done in hospitals. They may be planned in advance, like when you go in to have your tonsils out. Or they may be emergency operations, like having your appendix out.

This is the sort of adventure you may have if your appendix does have to be taken out.

JOHN HAS HAD A STOMACH-ACHE ALL NIGHT AND HAS BEEN SICK.

Where's the pain exactly, John?

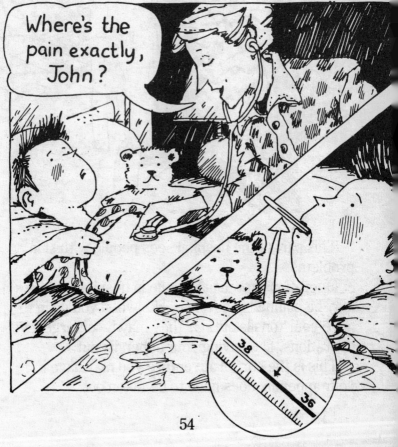

It's getting worse, Mum!

Can you come and see John quickly—please, doctor.

He'll need to go into hospital right away, Mrs Jones. He might need an operation to put things right.

WA...WA... WA...WA ...WA!

JOHN IS SEEN BY MORE DOCTORS AT THE HOSPITAL. THEY ARE CALLED SURGEON AND WILL DECIDE EXACTLY WHAT'S WRONG AND HOW TO PUT IT RIGHT.

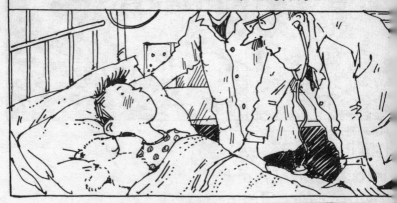

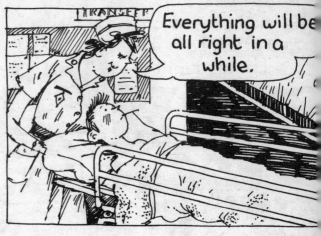

John needs a short operation He has appendicitis - part of his insides are inflamed. We'll have to take his appendix out.

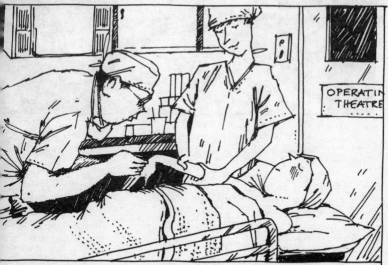

ANOTHER DOCTOR MAKES JOHN GO OFF TO SLEEP SO HE WON'T FEEL ANYTHING.

THE CHIEF SURGEON CAREFULLY REMOVES JOHN'S APPENDIX WHILE HE'S ASLEEP AND THEN STITCHES HIM UP.

IN LESS THAN AN HOUR JOHN IS BACK ON THE WARD, WAKING UP AND FEELING MUCH BETTER.

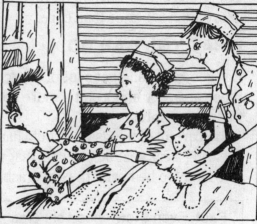

59

7 How to Stay Healthy

It is better to stop an illness coming than to try to put things right once they've gone wrong. There are lots of ways to do this. Remember, prevention is better than cure.

WHAT YOU CAN DO

Eat good food and get a lot of exercise. Both of these are very important – more about them in the next chapter.

Be careful of things that could harm you. Wearing a car seat belt means that you're much less likely to be hurt if the car crashes.

Fact. Even a low-speed car crash is like being dropped from a third-floor window on to concrete.

Head lice can be stamped out by combing your hair well every day. A comb breaks the legs of the lice so they can't lay eggs and carry on living in your hair. Motto: 'No legs means no eggs.'

Many infections like measles and mumps can be stopped by an injection. The injections get your body ready to fight the germs, and make sure you win! No one likes needles, but they are much better than being ill for days. Sometimes you can even eat special sugar lumps instead of having an injection.

Fact. 300 years ago prisoners would be let out of prison if they agreed to have a vaccination. This was the only way the first injections could be tested.

Cleaning your teeth stops them getting holes and needing fillings from the dentist. Tooth decay is the commonest disease in the world.

Fact. Dentists pull about four tonnes of teeth out of children's mouths every year. It almost makes you feel sorry for them – the dentists, not the children!

Washing hands after going to the toilet stops all kinds of germs spreading to you and your friends. A lot of stomach upsets can be prevented this way.

There are some worms that can live in the human body, a bit like the worms that live in the ground. Washing your hands will stop these getting into you too!

Fact. Dirty hands have millions of germs on them which are too small to see.

Coughs and sneezes really do spread diseases. Sneezing over someone is one very good way of spreading a cold.

> **Fact.** When you sneeze the air comes out at the speed of a hurricane. A hurricane with germs too! That's as fast as top tennis players hitting a tennis ball. Sneeze into a tissue or handkerchief instead.

Verrucas are spread when small germs called viruses get into the skin of your feet. If people with verrucas wear something on their feet – like rubber shoes in the swimming pool – then the virus can't spread to others.

> **Fact.** Verrucas are only warts that have been flattened by the weight of your body.

THE SENSES

The body can also look after itself. One way – or rather five ways – it does it is by taking in information from the five senses: SIGHT, TOUCH, TASTE, SMELL and HEARING.

The brain can use all this information to look after the body. So you can see trouble coming.

You know which foods taste good to eat.

Hearing and sight are both very important. That's why eye and ear tests are done so often

...OYWTHAHU!

once you start school. Any problems can be put right quickly before they get worse.

Sight is tested by asking you to read letters on a card. The letters get smaller and smaller. The doctor knows which ones you should be able to read. Most people will see the biggest ones, but if you need glasses, then you may not see the lower smaller letters. Each eye is tested in turn.

With hearing, there are machines that make different sounds which can be listened to through headphones. The doctor knows which ones you should be able to hear. As a matter of interest, most of you can hear much higher sounds than your parents, because your hearing is best when you are young.

Noise is measured in decibels (dBA).

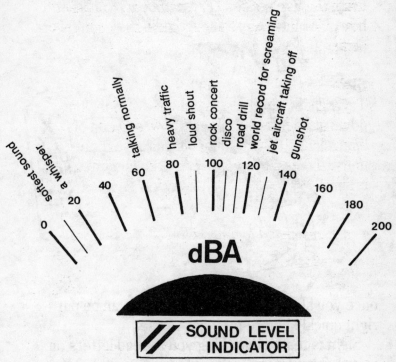

The other three senses – taste, smell and touch – are not tested at school because they don't often go wrong. The five senses all work together to send your brain useful information. It's very important for health that they all work properly.

> **Fact.** Butterflies can taste with their feet.
> Starfish have eyes on the ends of their arms.
> Snakes smell with their tongues.

Here are some ways you can 'fool' your brain
using the five senses. Try them out. You'll see
how difficult things can become if they don't work
perfectly.

Sight

Try walking along a straight line while looking
down at your feet through the wrong end of
binoculars. It's very difficult, because of the
unusual messages your eyes are sending to your
brain.

Experiment to find a blind spot in one eye

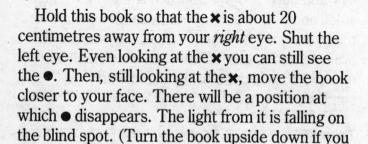

Hold this book so that the ✖ is about 20
centimetres away from your *right* eye. Shut the
left eye. Even looking at the ✖ you can still see
the ●. Then, still looking at the ✖, move the book
closer to your face. There will be a position at
which ● disappears. The light from it is falling on
the blind spot. (Turn the book upside down if you
want to find it in the other eye.)

Each eye normally helps the other, so that you don't realize there is one area in which each eye does not see. (This is because of a gap in the back of the eye where nerves run off to the brain.)

Taste

Cut a potato and an apple in similar slices. Close your eyes, pinch your nose shut and ask a friend to put each slice in turn into your mouth. Can you tell the difference? It's very hard to. The reason is that the sense of taste gets a great deal of help from the sense of smell.

You may have noticed that your nose is positioned very nicely right above your mouth – just the place to be to smell food. Many 'tastes' are in fact smells. That's why food appears to lose much of its taste when you have a blocked nose from a cold. In this experiment you are without the sense of sight too, because your eyes are closed.

Smell

Try and bore your brain with a smell. Find a nice smell and hold it under your nose. In quite a short time you won't be able to smell it any more. The brain seems to get fed up with a new smell fairly quickly. This is quite handy if you work somewhere smelly!

Touch

Cross your first and second fingers. Then put

your nose in the notch formed by the fingers. A lot of people think they are feeling two noses when they do this.

The reason is that the brain is getting touch messages from the outsides of the two fingers, and not the insides, which it quite reasonably

Move fingers up and down the nose

expects. Many people have their brain fooled by this trick. Try it yourself and see.

Question. Which place on your body can't you touch with your right hand? (The answer is given at the foot of the page.)

Hearing

Put a sea shell to your ear. (Anything with a similar shape will do if you can't find a shell.) Your ear will be fooled into hearing what sounds like the sea.

These are in fact normal, quiet sounds of your blood flowing inside your head.

Answer: Your right elbow.

8 Healthy Eating and Exercise

HEALTHY EATING

There is a saying that 'You are what you eat'. In a way this is true, because your body is made up of the food and drink you take in.

Food is needed for just three things:

1 Growth and repair of the body.

2 Energy to do things.

3 To keep the body healthy and well.

Growth and Repair

Growth and the repair of your body come from
the PROTEIN in food. Protein is found in foods
like meat, fish, eggs, milk, cereals and rice.
Proteins are important for growth as they make
up much of the cells of the body. These cells are
like the bricks that together make up a house.

Try this experiment to show growth in action.
Stand against a wall where a pencil or pen mark
will not matter and ask a grown-up to mark
across the top of your head. Put the date against
it. Do this every few months and you will see the
mark go higher and higher.

You will stop growing when you are about
eighteen. What you will be like then depends on
lots of things: how you look after yourself, what
your parents look like and what food you eat.

Energy

Energy for your body to do things comes from
CARBOHYDRATES (Car-Bo-Hy-Drates) and
FATS. Both these can build up in your body if
you eat too much and may make you overweight.

Different foods have different amounts of

energy in them. A bar of chocolate has about twenty times more energy in it than a stick of celery.

Carbohydrates are found in many foods, like bread and sugar. You are burning them up when you run around the playground.

There are different sorts of fat around. They are a very good energy food too. Butter and margarine, as well as cooking oils, are all fats. But beware, too much fat can build up in the body and make you overweight. This can stay with you and make for an unhealthy life when you are a grown-up.

> **Fact.** There's enough fat in a fully grown teacher to make seven bars of soap – some people who eat too much could make a lot more bars!

To Keep Healthy

VITAMINS, MINERALS and FIBRE are needed to keep you healthy.

Some things in food are there only in very small amounts, but they are vital for good health. That's why they are called VITAmins. When they were discovered, they were given letters of the alphabet as names.

Vitamin C is found in foods like fresh fruit. In olden days, before scientists knew about Vitamin C, sailors knew what happened if they went

70

without fresh fruit. They got a disease called
scurvy and their skin started bleeding and their
teeth fell out.

> **Fact.** In the sixteenth century diseases like
> scurvy killed more sailors than wars, storms
> and pirates put together.

Minerals like iron and calcium are just two of
the twenty needed by the body. Iron is used to
make blood, and is found in many foods, including
meat, eggs and cereals. Baked beans on toast has
quite a lot too! Milk is one of the best foods to
give your body calcium.

> **Fact.** There is enough iron in your body to
> make an iron nail.

Fibre is an important part of food even though
it goes straight through you. It gives your insides
something solid to work on. This means the food
moves easily through you.

It is important to get the balance right between all these things when you eat. This is called having a well-balanced diet.

Food Groups

You can think of a food as being in one of three groups.

1 Some it's best to take only small amounts of – Red Light.

2 Some are foods which you should go easy with – Orange Light.

3 Some you can eat as much of as you like – Green Light.

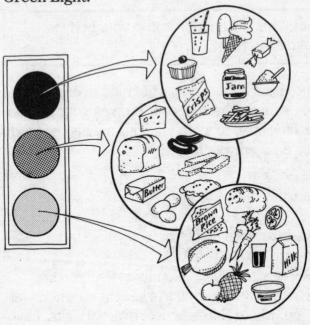

Red Light

Fried foods, sugar, sweets, ice cream and lollies, fizzy drinks, cakes, roast potatoes and chips, crisps and peanuts.

Orange Light

Cheese, eggs, white bread, fish fingers and fried fish, sausages and beefburgers, butter and margarine, and meat pies.

Green Light

Fresh fruit, cottage cheese, milk, white fish, salads, wholemeal bread, brown rice, jacket potatoes and fruit juice.

The way food is cooked makes a lot of difference. White fish is great food – a real Green Light part of the diet – but if it is fried in fat it gets an Orange Light.

Over-cooking foods like vegetables takes much of the goodness out. As a general rule, grilled food is better for you than fried food.

EXERCISE

Exercise is one of the best ways to look after your body. It keeps it strong and in good working order. It uses up fuel from food which otherwise could turn into rolls of fat.

Exercise should be a fun thing that you like doing. And it is important to keep it up when you grow up. Many illnesses, like heart attacks, have become more common nowadays, and lack of exercise is one reason why.

Walking, swimming, cycling and running are all good exercise. Some use more calories than others.

This is about what you could do on the energy in one bar of chocolate:

1 Run for twenty-five minutes.

2 Swim for thirty minutes.

3 Bicycle for forty minutes.

4 Sit in school lessons for three hours.

5 Watch TV for four hours.

6 Sleep for five hours.

Now you have an idea of which activities use most energy, arrange these in order of which burns up the most energy. (The answer is given at the foot of the page.)

1 Snow skiing.

2 Reading in bed.

3 Washing the dishes.

4 Disco dancing.

5 Walking to school.

Answer: 1, 4, 5, 3, 2.

Conclusion

Cavemen could expect to live to the age of eighteen, the Romans to the grand old age of twenty-two. Now our health is so much better, we can all expect to live a full life four times as long as this.

However, you must look after your body and your health. Your heart, for example, is the best pump around – far better than anything in a car or a fridge. But those machines can easily be repaired. Your heart will go for life without stopping and without any repairs – just as long as you look after it! So keep healthy and **well, well, well!**

Index

45.H

4/11900